National Novel Writing Month's Young Novelist Workbook

Elementary School
Fourth Edition

Created by National Novel Writing Month

Table of Contents

Hi, Young Writer!

Here it is, almost November, and you've decided to tackle one of the most fun and rewarding challenges ever: writing a novel in one month. Before you begin, we want to give you a super high five just for showing up!

You may be wondering how you will go about writing a novel in a month. Isn't novel writing just for famous authors? The answer, our friends, is no! Anyone can write a novel. You just have to have a few ideas, some paper, and a pen. It's as easy as that!

Writing a novel is kind of like building a Lego spaceship from scratch: when the pieces are spread out on the ground, the job seems impossible. But if you work piece by piece, before you know it, you've built an entire ship! By breaking any big job into smaller jobs, you'll find that anything is possible.

If you're still not sure, we've put together this nifty workbook to help you come up with some novel ideas for November. You'll get to create characters that are out of this world, build cities with the power of your imagination, and come up with a story that is exciting enough to write about for 30 days straight! We have lots of really cool activities to get you writing and keep you writing during NaNoWriMo.

This November you will be doing a brave and wonderful thing: you'll be giving yourself a goal, and you'll be setting out to achieve it. And no matter how things turn out in the end—whether you finish your book or you don't—it is jaw-droppingly cool that you set out to write a novel in just one month. And for that, we salute you.

Good luck, from all of us here at NaNoWriMo. May your writing adventure be a great one!

The NaNoWriMo Team

How To
Write a Book

Putting Away Your Inner Editor

Before you begin your noveling adventure, you want to put your Inner Editor somewhere where he or she can't pester you. Your Inner Editor is the one who tells you when you misspell something or when you don't use the right punctuation. A lot of the time, your Inner Editor is there to help you write well. But if your Inner Editor gets grumpy, he or she can be pretty mean. He or she may tell you that your sentences aren't good enough, and that you are not a good writer. And NaNoWriMo puts your Inner Editor in a really bad mood, since you will be ignoring a lot of what he or she is trying to tell you. During November, don't be surprised if your Inner Editor tries to get you to erase everything and start over almost every day.

This is why it is important to put your Inner Editor away for a month. The point of National Novel Writing Month is to explore your imagination and just write. Every word counts, no matter if it is misspelled or completely made up. In order to avoid erasing, you'll need to put your Inner Editor away. You can bring him back in December, but for now, your Inner Editor needs to be sent away on vacation.

In the space below, draw your Inner Editor. Is your Inner Editor a girl or a boy? Does he or she look mean? What is he or she wearing? Remember to use a lot of color and details.

After you draw your Inner Editor, cut him or her out and put him or her away!

> **Some places to put your Inner Editor:**
>
> - Under your bed.
>
> - At the bottom of your dirty clothes hamper.
>
> - In an old shoe box in your closet.
>
> - Tucked away in the back of your junk drawer.
>
> - Locked in your teacher's desk.
>
> - In a locked safe (if you or someone you know has one).
>
> - Buried in a time capsule in your backyard.

You can even give him to a friend or family member for safekeeping. Whatever you do, do not keep him or her anywhere near your desk or wherever you like to write. In November, if you feel the need to erase, start over, or quit, remember that it is your Inner Editor shouting from where he or she is hidden. The further your Inner Editor is from you, the better.

What Makes a Novel a Novel?

You've received the scary news that you're going to write a novel. But what does that mean, exactly? What is a novel, anyway?

A **novel** is a long story containing made-up characters and events. A novel may have many chapters, but all the chapters focus on the same story.

Think of books you have read recently. Which were novels? **Choose one of those novels, preferably one that you really liked a lot or just know inside and out. Write the name of that book and its author here:**

A Novel I Love:

_____ ,

by _____

Think of that book as a model you can use when you get stuck. You never want to copy it, but you can always look to it for ideas.

Now take out the novel you chose and fill in the blanks below.

1. How do you know this book is a novel?

_____

_____

_____

_____

2. Who are the important characters in this book?

_____

_____

_____

_____

3. What is the story mostly about?

_____

_____

_____

_____

4. Where and when does it take place?

_____

_____

_____

5. Why should someone else read this novel?

_____

_____

_____

_____

Now you're ready to present your novel to classmates. Don't worry; you don't have to give a full book report. Instead, create an advertisement for it! Start with a short summary of your novel including the title, author, and a sentence or two explaining what the story is mostly about. (Don't give away the ending.) Most importantly, though, try to make classmates want to read it.

Check out this example:

James and the Giant Peach, by Roald Dahl, is the story of what happens to a boy named James after he goes to live with two mean aunts. James meets a strange man and after that, everything changes. A huge peach grows in his yard and soon he and the peach take off on a truly amazing adventure!

After reading this ad, you know the basics of *James and the Giant Peach*: its title, its author, its main character, and what the story is mostly about. But perhaps you want to know more. Who was the mysterious man? Why did a huge peach grow in James's yard? What was James' adventure? Perhaps you are curious enough to read *James and the Giant Peach* for yourself!

Below, prepare your own ad for the novel you wrote about above. And remember: Try to make classmates want to read the book!

_____

_____

_____

_____

_____

_____

_____

Great Book, Gross Book

Out of all the books you've read in your life, there were some that were a ton of fun to read and some that were a lot like going to the dentist on your birthday. Before you start writing your own story, it's helpful to write down what, to you, makes a book "great" (interesting, exciting, and fun to read) and what makes a book "gross" (boring, sad, and un-fun to read).

Great Book

Let's start by writing a list of books you liked reading. In the spaces below, write down the title and author of three books you like:

1. Title _____

   Author _____

2. Title _____

   Author _____

3. Title _____

   Author _____

8

Now, make a list of everything you can think of that made those books so amazing! Did the author include lots of funny details? Did the main character remind you of someone you really like? Your list can include anything from "happy endings" to "talking animals."

_____

_____

_____

_____

_____

_____

_____

Once you have finished this list, keep it with you at all times during November. As you try to figure out what kind of book you'll write in November, take a long look at this list you just made—all the ingredients for a great story are in there.

Gross Book

Now, think about all those books and stories you've read or started to read that you would rather eat a mayonnaise, peanut butter, and onion sandwich than read again. In the spaces below, list the title and author of three books you did not like.

1. Title _____

   Author _____

2. Title _____

   Author _____

3. Title _____

   Author _____

Now, write a list of things that made these books not very much fun to read. Was the plot totally boring? Were the characters impossible to believe or to like? Again, this list can include anything from " too many bad guys" to "too many wizards."

_____

_____

_____

_____

_____

_____

_____

_____

Just like the list of things you love in a story, keep this list with you at all times during November. It might seem silly to have to remind yourself of the things you dislike, but the things on this list are pretty sneaky. They might end up in your story if you don't keep a close eye on them.

Create Awesome Characters

Most people think that an action-packed story makes a book fun to read, but in order to have an exciting story, you need to have really interesting characters.

Boring Characters vs. Awesome Characters

Boring Character: A girl named Maggie

Awesome Character: A girl named Maggie who can walk through walls, read other people's minds, has a pet giraffe named Phil, was born on the planet Yumip, and has just learned that she comes from a family of magicians.

Not only are interesting characters fun to read about, they are also fun to write about. The three characters you will be writing about this November are the main character, the supporting character, and the villain.

The Main Character
The main character is the person, animal, or thing that has the starring role. In most stories, the main character is on a journey to get something he or she wants more than anything in the world, whether it is to slay a dragon, join the circus, or win the national taco-eating contest!

The Supporting Character
A supporting character is someone who helps the main character along the way. A supporting character is kind of like a sidekick—he or she helps the main character achieve his or her goal, like winning that taco-eating contest we just mentioned.

The Villain
The villain is—you guessed it—the "bad guy" (or gal!) in your novel. The villain wants to make sure the main character does not succeed.

Okay, let's get started in creating some awesome characters. And remember, your characters can be anything or anyone you want them to be—monkeys from Mars, talking plates and spoons, or people just like you. This is your novel, and you're in charge!

Author's name _____   Character's name _____

Main Character Worksheet

Let's start by answering some questions about your main character. This character is the most important one in your novel. You will write a lot about this character in November, so make sure he or she is someone you want to spend a lot of time with.

Answer the following questions about your main character. Remember to use lots of details!

1. What is your main character's name?

_____

2. How old is your main character?

_____

3. What is your main character? A person? An animal? A talking lampshade?

_____

_____

_____

4. What does your main character look like? Is there anything different or interesting about the way he or she looks?

_____

_____

_____

_____

_____

5. Where does your main character live? Does he or she like it there?

_____

_____

_____

_____

_____

Draw your main character in the box below. Include important details like his or her hair, clothes, shoes, and what expression is on his or her face. Be sure to include as many details as you can, and don't forget to use lots of color.

If you want to get to know this character even better, answer more questions about him or her. The more you know about your characters, the better!

6. What does your main character do for fun?

_____

_____

_____

_____

_____

7. What is your main character's favorite food?

_____

_____

8. Favorite movie?

_____

_____

9. Favorite TV show?

_____

_____

10. Favorite band or song?

_____

_____

11. Favorite book?

_____

_____

12. What can your main character do better than anyone else?

_____

_____

_____

_____

_____

13. What makes your main character happy after a bad day?

_____

_____

_____

_____

14. What makes your main character angry?

_____

_____

_____

_____

_____

15. What makes him or her sad?

_____

_____

_____

_____

16. What is your main character's family like? Describe them.

_____

_____

_____

_____

Super Bonus Questions

Here are even more questions to answer about your main character if you are up for it.

17. What's one secret your main character has never told anyone?

_____

_____

_____

18. Is your main character fun to be around? Is he or she shy? What do people think when they first meet your main character?

_____

_____

_____

_____

19. What do you really like about your main character?

_____

_____

_____

_____

20. What don't you like about your main character?

_____

_____

_____

_____

_____

21. Describe your main character in three words:

1. _____

2. _____

3. _____

22. Where would your main character go on his or her dream vacation?

_____

_____

_____

_____

_____

23. What does his or her bedroom look like? Is there anything hanging on the walls? Is it clean or messy?

_____

_____

_____

_____

_____

24. What is the best thing that ever happened to your main character?

_____

_____

_____

_____

25. What is the worst thing that ever happened to your main character?

_____

_____

_____

_____

26. If your main character won the lottery, what would he or she do with the money?

_____

_____

_____

_____

_____

_____

Supporting Character Worksheet

Most novels have more than one supporting character, including a few friends, some family members, and maybe even the other kids at the main character's school. All of these people might play important roles in helping the main character along the way. For now, though, it is best to pick one major supporting character and focus on him or her first. You can always add more supporting characters in November as you write your novel!

Answer the following questions about your supporting character. Remember to use lots of details!

1. What is your supporting character's name?

_____

2. How old is your supporting character?

_____

3. What is your supporting character? A person? An animal? A robot?

_____

_____

4. How does the supporting character know the main character? Is he or she a friend? A family member? How did they first meet?

_____

_____

_____

_____

_____

5. What does your supporting character look like? Is there anything different or interesting about how he or she looks?

_____

_____

_____

_____

6. Where does your supporting character live? Does he or she like it there?

_____

_____

_____

_____

Draw your supporting character in the box below. Include important details like his or her hair, clothes, shoes, and what expression is on his or her face. Be sure to include as many details as you can, and don't forget to use lots of color.

Bonus Questions

If you want to get to know this character even better, answer more questions about him or her. The more you know about your characters, the better!

7. What does your supporting character do for fun?

_____

_____

_____

_____

_____

8. What is your supporting character's favorite food?

_____

_____

9. Favorite movie?

_____

_____

10. Favorite TV show?

_____

_____

11. Favorite band or song?

_____

_____

12. Favorite book?

_____

_____

13. What can your supporting character do better than anyone else?

_____

_____

_____

_____

14. What makes your supporting character happy after a bad day?

_____

_____

_____

_____

15. What makes your supporting character angry?

_____

_____

_____

_____

16. What makes him or her sad?

_____

_____

_____

_____

17. What is your supporting character's family like? Describe them.

_____

_____

_____

_____

Super Bonus Questions

Here are even more questions to answer about this character if you are up for it!

18. What's one secret your supporting character has never told anyone?

_____

_____

_____

19. Is your supporting character fun to be around? Is he or she shy? What do people think when they first meet your supporting character?

_____

_____

_____

_____

20. What do you really like about your supporting character?

_____

_____

_____

21. What don't you like about your supporting character?

_____

_____

_____

_____

_____

22. Describe your supporting character in three words:

1. _____

2. _____

3. _____

23. What annoys your supporting character more than anything else?

_____

_____

_____

_____

_____

24. Where would your supporting character go on his or her dream vacation?

_____

_____

_____

_____

_____

25. What does his or her bedroom look like?

_____

_____

_____

_____

_____

26. What is the best thing that ever happened to your supporting character?

_____

_____

_____

_____

_____

27. What is the worst thing that ever happened to your supporting character?

_____

_____

_____

_____

_____

28. If your supporting character won the lottery, what would he or she do with the money?

_____

_____

_____

_____

_____

Author's name _____   Character's name _____

Villain Worksheet

Finally, it is time to answer questions about your villain. Believe it or not, you should know just as much about your villain as you do all your other characters. Okay, here we go!

Answer the following questions about your villain!

1. What is your villain's name?

_____

2. How old is your villain?

_____

3. What is your villain? A person? An animal? A fire-breathing ball of lint?

_____

_____

4. What does your villain look like? Is there anything interesting or different about the way he or she looks?

_____

_____

_____

_____

_____

5. What is your villain's greatest weakness? What would be one way to defeat him or her?

_____

_____

_____

_____

6. Where does your villain live? Does he or she like it there?

_____

_____

_____

_____

Draw your villain here. Include important details like his or her hair, clothes, shoes, and what expression is on his or her face. Be sure to include as many details as you can, and don't forget to use lots of color.

Bonus Questions

If you want to get to know this character even better, answer more questions about him or her. The more you know about your characters, the better!

7. What does your villain do for fun?

_____

_____

_____

_____

_____

8. What is your villain's favorite food?

_____

_____

9. Favorite movie?

_____

_____

10. Favorite TV show?

_____

_____

11. Favorite band or song?

_____

_____

12. Favorite book?

_____

_____

13. What can your villain do better than anyone else?

_____

_____

_____

_____

14. What makes your villain happy after a bad day?

_____

_____

_____

_____

15. What makes your villain angry?

_____

_____

_____

_____

_____

16. What makes him or her sad?

_____

_____

_____

_____

17. What is your villain's family like? Describe them.

_____

_____

_____

_____

Super Bonus Questions

Here are even more questions to answer about this character if you are up for it!

18. What's one secret your villain has never told anyone?

_____

_____

_____

19. Is your villain scary? Mean? What do people think when they first meet your villain?

_____

_____

_____

20. Is there anything likeable about your villain? Does he or she have a soft spot or a good side?

_____

_____

_____

21. What do you dislike most about your villain's dreadful ways?

_____

_____

_____

_____

_____

22. Describe your villain in three words:

      1. _____

      2. _____

      3. _____

23. What annoys your villain more than anything else?

_____

_____

_____

_____

_____

24. Where would your villain go on his or her dream vacation?

_____

_____

_____

_____

25. What does his or her bedroom look like?

_____

_____

_____

_____

26. What is the best thing that ever happened to your villain?

_____

_____

_____

_____

27. What is the worst thing that ever happened to your villain?

_____

_____

_____

_____

28. If your villain won the lottery, what would he or she do with the money?

_____

_____

_____

_____

- -

Just so you know, you don't have to include all of the worksheet information in your novel if you don't want to. But the more you know about your characters, the easier it will be to bring them to life in your novel.

Now that you have some really interesting characters, it's time to figure out what is going happen in your novel.

Get ready, because the adventure is just beginning!

Make Up Your Story

Okay, so you know who your characters are. That's terrific! Now it is time to figure out what they are going to do this November. **Most stories are about the adventures a main character has on the way to making his or her dreams come true.** Whether the quest is to become the king of a secret world under the bed, or to be the first person to land on Jupiter, the journey is never easy. Your character will encounter many obstacles along the way, and that is a good thing. These obstacles are what make a story exciting!

Imagine a story about someone who wants a microwavable pizza more than anything in the world. How boring would the story be if all this character had to do was walk from his or her bedroom to the kitchen and pop the pizza in the microwave? That story is so uneventful it can be told in just one sentence. If this same character is afraid of the dark and has to walk down a pitch-black hallway to get to the kitchen and, once there, battle a villainous monkey-ninja who is hogging all the microwavable pizzas...Now, that's more like it!

If you have filled out your **character worksheets**, you already know a lot about your characters.

Now we are going to answer some big questions about:

1. What your main character wants.

2. What he or she needs to do to make those dreams come true.

Fill in the blanks below. You may want to take out and review your character worksheets as you work!

More than anything in the world, my main character, _____,
(main character's name)

wants _____

42

_____

_____

_____

In order to get what he/she wants, my main character has to go on a journey to

_____

_____

_____

_____

But the journey won't be easy. My character has to overcome his/her fear of

_____

Plus, the no-good villain _____ is doing everything in
                                          (villain's name)

his/her power to stop my main character from getting what he/she wants by

_____

_____

_____

But, my main character has a great friend named _____
                                                          (supporting character's name)

who is helping him/her along the way by _____

_____

_____

In the end, my main character and supporting character defeat the villain by (Hint: Check out question number 5 on your "Villain Worksheet". If your villain has a weakness, this may be a way your main character can defeat him or her.)

_____

_____

_____

_____

_____

Bonus Exercise: Your Villain's Story

Try answering the following questions about your villain. Your bad guys and gals have dreams of their own, and it will help make your story even better if you know what those are.

> If your main character is trying to make the world's largest burrito, it may be helpful to know your villain's dream of a world free of burritos due to his fear of pinto beans.

What does your villain want more than anything else in the world? Is it defeating the main character? Taking over the world? Or something else?

_____

_____

_____

_____

What is the one thing your villain is afraid of more than anything else? Is it your main character? Or something unexpected like furry kittens?

_____

_____

_____

Super Bonus Exercise: Your Supporting Character's Story

Add even more twists and turns to your story by answering the following questions about your supporting character. He or she might have some dreams and fears of his or her own.

> If your main character wants to travel to the planet Zorbot for their famous french fries, perhaps your supporting character is coming along to finally see the universe's largest gumball that is also located there. There is a problem, though. Your supporting character is afraid of space travel!

What does your supporting character want more than anything else in the world? To see the main character make his or her dreams come true? Or does this supporting character have his or her own dreams?

_____

_____

_____

_____

What is the one thing your supporting character is afraid of more than anything else?

_____

_____

_____

_____

Congratulations! You have a great story. Now all you have to do is fill in all the details about how your characters will get from the beginning of the story to the end. You can figure out a lot of these details before November by outlining your plot in the next worksheet.

Outline Your Plot

If you filled out the last worksheet, you probably have an idea of what kind of adventure your characters are going on this November. You know that your main character is going to embark on a journey to make his or her dreams come true along with your supporting character, and they are not going to let that pesky villain get in the way. So, now it is time to take the next step and map out how that is all going to happen.

You may be wondering how you get from the beginning of your novel to the end. Well, it is not as hard as you think once you have a plan. Most stories follow the same outline and this outline is known as the **plot**. See the picture below.

This is the **Plot Rollercoaster.** This Plot Rollercoaster will help you understand all the sections below.

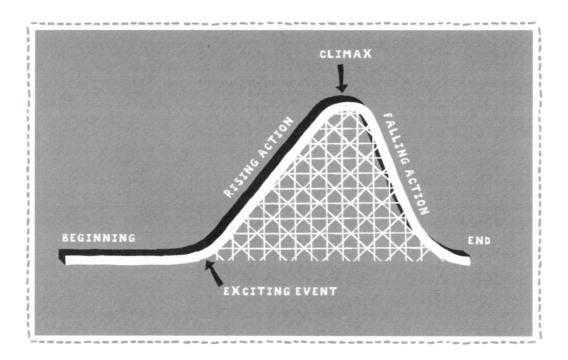

The Beginning

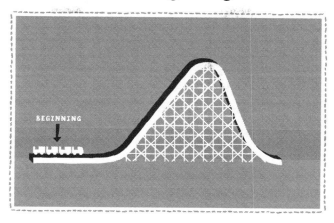

What kind of rollercoaster are we riding?

Most books you read start by telling the reader a little bit about the characters, the setting, and the story. Just like you might want to know just how scary or wimpy a rollercoaster is before you get in line, someone who is going to read your story will want to know a little bit about what kind of book he or she is about to read.

The beginning of *Boris the Unicorn*

Boris the Unicorn is in his bedroom playing *Dance Dance Revolution* and eating a plate of mini-pizzas. Boris knows that DDR is old-fashioned, but he doesn't care. It's his favorite game of all-time.

Boris is a young unicorn with messy hair and a messy room covered with wall-to-wall video-game posters, video-game magazines, and every video-game console known to man. His mom, Wilma, walks into his room with another plate of mini-pizzas.

"Mom, I'm *soooo* bored," Boris says, nearly knocking the plate of mini-pizzas out of his mom's hands as he dances.

Wilma looks at him and shakes her head. "That doesn't make any sense at all. You have every video game in the world! You sure look like you're having fun."

"How many times do we have to go over this, Mom!" Boris exclaims. "I wanna join the circus. I wanna hang out with the clowns, the trapeze artists, the elephants . . ."

He stops dancing and slumps onto the edge of his bed. "Boris, you know that unicorns have been banned from the circus by that evil ringmaster, Ivan." Wilma hands him the plate of pizza. "Plus, how will you live without me, your mini-pizzas, and all this stuff. You get homesick when you go to Archie's house for two hours!"

Okay, that was a good beginning. We've met the main character and been introduced to the story: Boris wants to join the circus, but he is afraid to leave home. And the villain, Ivan, has forbidden unicorns to join the circus.

In the space below, write three sentences of your own beginning. Introduce your characters, setting, and your story. This does not have to be perfect. You just want to get an idea of what you might include in your beginning when we start writing for real in November.

_____

_____

_____

_____

_____

_____

_____

Okay, great! Now it's time for some action!

The Exciting Event

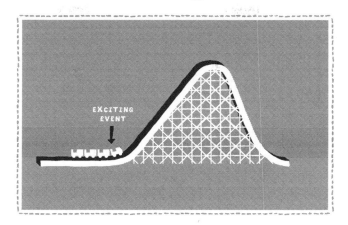

Getting on the Rollercoaster

The exciting event is something exciting that happens to your main character which launches him or her into the adventure whether he or she likes it or not. It can be a pretty scary moment for your main character. He or she needs to get on that rollercoaster no matter how frightening it might look. Once your main character is on, there's no turning back.

Here is the exciting event that happens in this story:

Boris is looking through the new video game releases at his favorite store, Gamer Heaven. He sees his friend, Archie the Chinchilla, at the counter.

"Hey Archie, have you played the new *Super Mario Kart* yet?" Boris asks.

"No time for video games, my friend. Been practicing my one-man-band act for the tryouts this Saturday. I just came here to sell my old games for a bus ticket," Archie says, jumping up and down with excitement.

"What do you mean? What tryouts? A bus ticket for what?" Boris looks worried.

"I'm trying out for the circus, my man," Archie says, as if it were the most normal thing to do in the world. "I need the bus ticket to get out to Springfield, where they're held. Oh, and get this, I have some extra cash from selling my old PS2 console, so I can buy you a ticket. It would be super cool if you came with me."

"I would, but aren't unicorns banned from the circus?" Boris says. He looks down at the ground.

"I've heard that," Archie says. He does not look worried about it one bit. "If you're good enough, they have to let you join! I'll be at your house tomorrow at 8 AM sharp, so be ready."

If an **exciting event** never happened to Boris, he would more than likely continue to eat pizza and play video games in his bedroom. This might sound like a pretty fun life to live, but it is not a very fun life to read about.

In three sentences, describe the event that causes your main character to begin his or her adventure. Does your supporting character help your main character get going? Or does something else happen to your main character to get him or her out of a rut and into action?

_____

_____

_____

_____

_____

_____

Rising Action

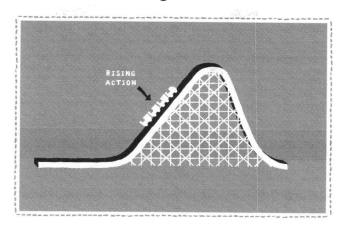

Climbing the Big Hill

The **rising action** will be the longest part of your story. You will write all about your characters and what happens to them during their adventure. Think about your book as a really tall rollercoaster—the higher you go, the more exciting it gets. This part is made up of many events, each of them building and building to the most exciting part of your story, the **climax**.

Here is a list of things that happen during the rising action in our made-up novel, **Boris the Unicorn:**

1. Archie arrives at Boris' house on the day of the tryouts. Boris says goodbye to his mom (she baked him some mini-pizzas for the road), and he tries not to look back to his room where he imagines his video games waving farewell. Boris finally hugs his mom and runs out the door.

2. As soon as they get to the tryouts, Boris is glad he chose to come. They meet all kinds of interesting people, animals, and magical creatures. It is like a party all day long! Archie and he have a blast talking to everyone and making new friends.

3. When it is Boris' turn to get up in front of the evil ringmaster and actually try out for the circus, Boris realizes that he doesn't know any circus tricks at all. He tries to think of what he is good at, and all he can think of is that he is good

at playing video games. He is about to give up and walk off the stage, when he hears his friend Archie yell from the audience.

"*Dance Dance Revolution!*" he hollers.

That is it! All those hours spent playing *Dance Dance Revolution* have made Boris an amazing dancer.

Just then, the circus band begins to play, and Boris starts to dance. He is amazing, and everyone cheers—everyone except Ivan. Nothing was going to change his mind.

"No unicorns in the circus!" Ivan says, "unless they're flipping burgers at the food stand!"

"What about friends of unicorns!?" Archie yells out from the crowd.

"Yes, that includes their friends!" Ivan returns.

 4.   Boris and Archie are not going to give up on their dream to become circus stars. They take the jobs at the food stand flipping burgers, but they have a plan.

Every night, right before closing time, Boris gets up on the food counter and dances, while Archie plays music using pots, pans, spoons, and anything else he finds lying around the kitchen.

They are so good that it isn't long before Archie and Boris have a following. Even Ivan appears to enjoy the act and invites them to perform for one night only on the main stage.

Boris and Archie can hardly believe their ears when the ringmaster asks them to perform. Little do they know that Ivan has an awful plan up his sleeve.

In the space below, describe up to four events that may be included in your rising action. Don't forget to include your supporting characters!

1.

2.

_____

_____

_____

3.

_____

_____

_____

4.

_____

_____

_____

And then . . . .

The Climax

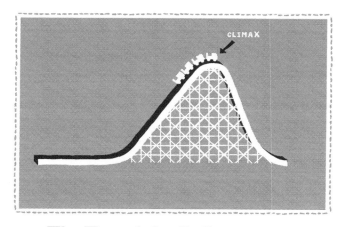

The Top of the Rollercoaster

The **climax** is the moment where things get **really** exciting. The villain appears out of the blue, the lottery is won, and the audience gasps. This is the moment at the very tippy-top of the rollercoaster, right before your high-speed drop! This moment doesn't last long. It can be as short as one paragraph—just enough to make your readers hold their breath in suspense and ask, "What's going to happen next?!"

> ### Here is an example of a climax:
>
> It's finally the big night and the main circus tent is packed with people. The air is filled with the smell of popcorn and hotdogs and the sound of laughter.
>
> Boris and Archie make their grand entrance onstage, and the crowd goes wild. As soon as they begin their act, Ivan approaches close behind them with a bucket of oil and dumps it all over the floor beneath Boris' hooves. Archie spots Ivan.
>
> "Boris! Watch out!" he yells.

In the space below, write three sentences describing what might happen in your book's climax. It does not have to be long, but it should be exciting!

_____

_____

_____

_____

_____

_____

The Falling Action

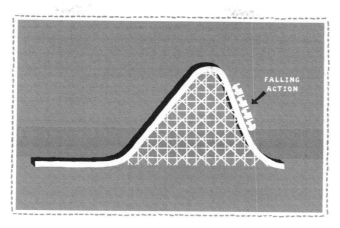

Speeding Down the Tracks

The **falling action** is the fast-paced, super action-packed part of your novel. You are finally speeding down the tracks of the rollercoaster with your hands in the air! Does the villain get defeated? Do the main character's dreams finally come true? If so, how?

Here is an example of falling action:

Boris jumps out of the way of the approaching oil spill. Archie leaps across the stage and tackles Ivan. A few of the clowns that were hanging out backstage grab Ivan and tie him to a chair. The crowd cheers, and all the circus performers come up on stage to give Archie high fives and hugs. Others work hard to clean up the oil spill.

"Finally, someone stood up to him! Hooray for Archie!" the bearded woman exclaims.

"Hooray is right! Archie, you are the hero of the day!" Boris said. "You are one quick chinchilla, and an even better best friend."

"Hey, it was nothing." Archie says. "What do you say we get back on that stage and drive the crowd crazy?"

"Let's do it!" Boris says, and they run back on stage to meet the crowd.

Write three sentences about how your characters defeat the villain! Make sure this part is packed with exciting action. You already answered a question about how your main character might defeat your villain on your "Create Your Story" worksheet, so it may be helpful to pull this worksheet out and read it before you write your falling action below.

_____

_____

_____

_____

_____

_____

_____

The Ending

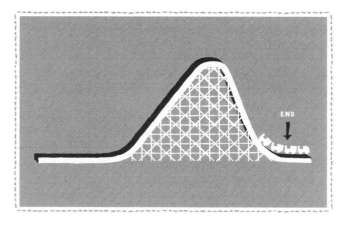

Getting Off the Rollercoaster

This is how things work out in the very end. This is when your main character really knows that his or her dream has come true. The rollercoaster ride is over, and they get to think about how much fun the ride has been.

An example of an ending:

Archie starts playing a harmonica, guitar, foot drum, and a slide whistle all at the same time, and Boris starts to dance. The crowd goes wild.

Boris sees his mom in the audience with a whole plate of hot mini-pizzas. For a moment, he thinks about jumping off the stage and running over to her. But he thinks again, and keeps dancing. His dream had finally come true. The mini-pizzas could wait.

How might your story end? Write three sentences about what will happen after your main character's dreams come true!

Your Own Plot Rollercoaster!

Now that you have an outline for your novel, you can fill out the Plot Rollercoaster on page 61. Before you do, check out the Plot Roller Coatser for *Boris the Unicorn* on the next page.

The Parts of the Plot Rollercoaster:

1. **The Beginning:** What kind of rollercoaster are we riding?

2. **The Exciting Incident:** Getting on the rollercoaster

3. **The Rising Action:** Climbing up the big hill

4. **The Climax:** The top of the rollercoaster

5. **The Falling Action:** Speeding down the tracks

6. **The Ending:** Getting off the rollercoaster

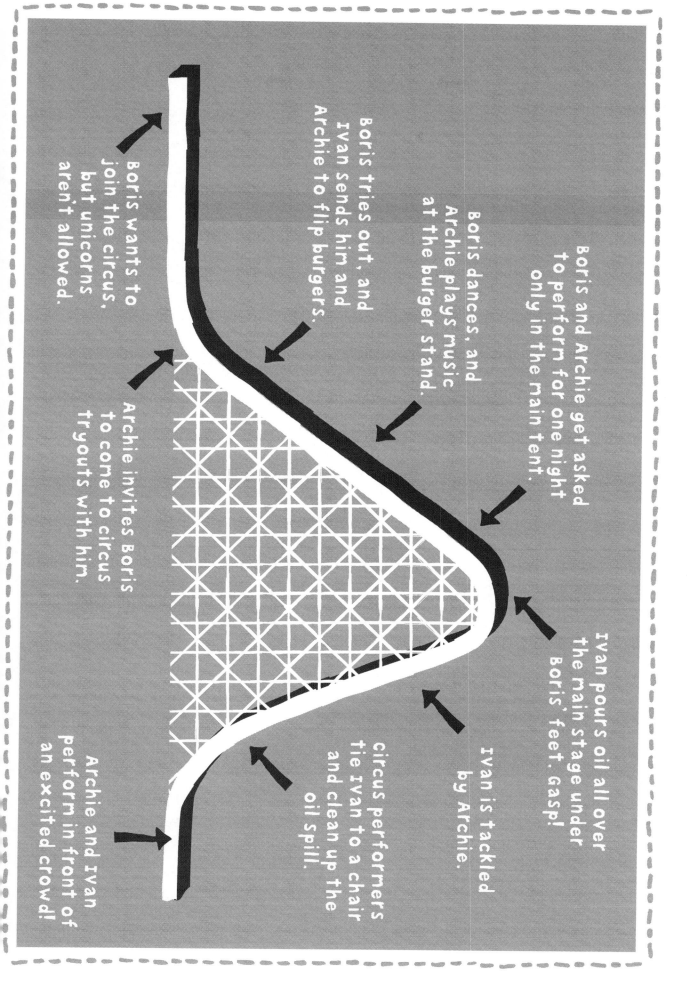

Boris wants to join the circus, but unicorns aren't allowed.

Archie invites Boris to come to circus tryouts with him.

Boris and Archie get asked to perform for one night only in the main tent.

Boris dances, and Archie plays music at the burger stand.

Boris tries out, and Ivan sends him and Archie to flip burgers.

Ivan pours oil all over the main stage under Boris' feet. Gasp!

Ivan is tackled by Archie.

circus performers tie Ivan to a chair and clean up the oil spill.

Archie and Ivan perform in front of an excited crowd!

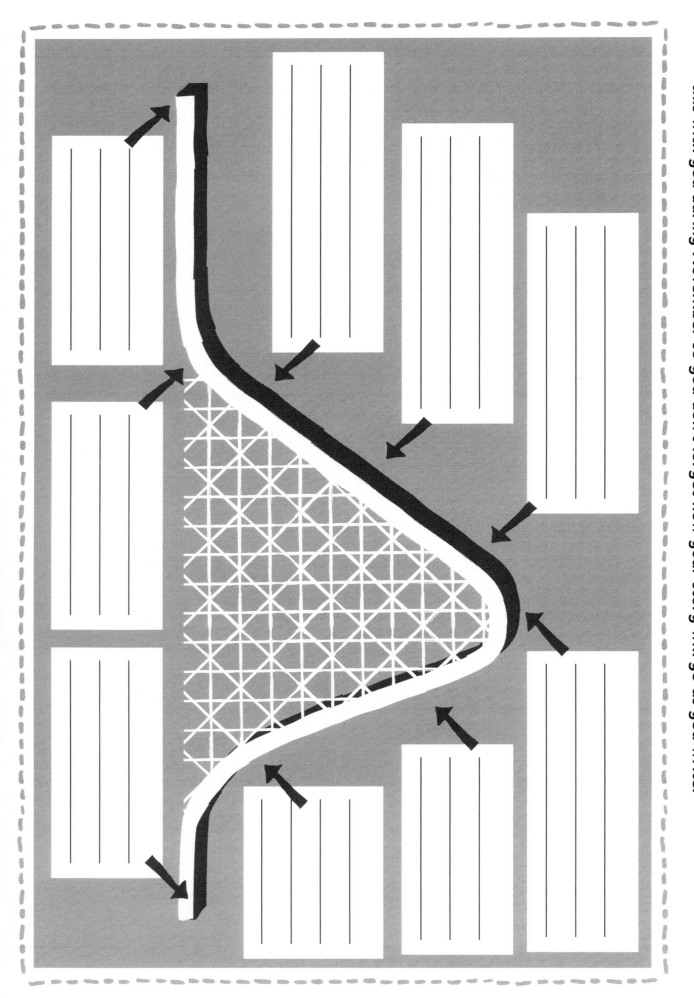

Fill in the blanks on your plot rollercoaster. As you can see, there's not much space to write for each section. Just write down the most important idea for each section, using as few words as possible. Keep this with you during November so you don't forget how your story will go as you write!

Map Your Setting

Now that you have a cast of characters and ideas about your plot, you probably have an idea of where and when your story is set. For example, if your main character is a Martian who sets out to find the planet Zorbot, your story is probably set in outer space in the future. Or maybe your main character is like Boris, in which case your novel would be set at the circus today. This is a great start, but now it's time to add all the really interesting details!

It is important to know all that you can about your setting. Just like characters, settings are much more exciting if they're described with tons of detail.

A boring setting: "Joe lived in a house long ago"

An exciting setting: "Long before there were computers, televisions, or even toothbrushes, Joe lived in a 120-room orange mansion next to a Pegasus zoo."

Now that's a setting we want to read more about!

We've given you some space below to map out your setting. You'll have the chance to draw all the different kinds of settings in your novel, from your main character's house on a sunny day to the most villainous room in your villain's house during a terrible lightning storm. Take your time, have fun, and don't forget the details!

Draw the map of the town or planet or universe where your story takes place. Include details that show when your story takes place, too.

Draw your main character's house.

Draw your main character's bedroom.

Draw your supporting character's house.

Draw your supporting character's bedroom.

Draw your villain's house.

Draw the most villainous room in your villain's house.

Draw your main character's favorite place to hang out when he or she is not battling the villain.

Draw the place where the final showdown between your main character and villain happens!

Bonus Exercise

If you liked drawing your settings, and want to keep working, go back and add even more details! Add trees, park benches, poisonous cactus plants, icebergs, rollercoasters, and Ferris wheels! Feel free to get crazy! If your town suddenly has a lake filled with lime Jell-O, that's great! That is just the kind of detail that will make your story more fun to write... and to read.

How to Write Really Good Dialogue

You've got some awesome characters, an action-packed plot, and a setting like no other! You're doing great! All that's left is learning how to write really good dialogue!

Dialogue is what two or more characters say to each other. The exact words they speak are put between quotation marks. We experience dialogue all the time in our everyday lives. Here's some dialogue you might hear on any given day:

"Hey, dude. How are you?" John said.

"I'm really good. Thanks for asking. And you?" Sam said.

"Good, thanks," John said.

Of course, this kind of dialogue is really important to everyday life. If we didn't say hello and ask people how they were doing, we might lose a lot of friends, fast. But in books, this kind of daily dialogue is boring.

Dialogue should:

1. Move your story forward

2. Help someone who is reading your book get to know your characters better

Dialogue that moves your story forward:

"Captain, we've spotted something on the horizon!" Pirate Willy yelled, pressing the binoculars to his eyes.

The Captain ran up to him, snatching the binoculars out of Willy's hands. "That's impossible!"

The Captain immediately saw that Pirate Willy was right. There was something on the horizon. And it was gaining on them.

The Captain cursed and shouted to his crew, "Full sail! We have to outrun them!"

This dialogue has our attention right from the start! As readers, we're already asking the questions: What did the pirate spot on the horizon? Are the pirates going to get out alive? We want to know what happens next. If the writer had spent three pages going back and forth between Willy and the Captain about how delicious breakfast was, by the time we got to the mysterious thing on the horizon, we'd already be asleep.

Also notice that dialogue follows special rules for punctuation and capitalization. A character's exact words are put inside quotation marks. Also, each new quote starts with a capital letter. As you write, be sure to follow the rules used here.

Dialogue Tags Other Than "Said"

agreed

answered

argued

asked

begged

complained

cried

giggled

hinted

hissed

howled

interrupted

laughed

lied

mumbled

nagged

promised

questioned

Dialogue that helps readers get to know your characters:

"Excuse me young man," Mark said, awkwardly. "But what is that thing you're pressing into your ear? Is it some kind of futuristic robot?"

Greg, who was talking on his cell phone, looked up at Mark, annoyed.

"It's my phone, dude! What planet are you from?"

"I am from planet Earth," Mark said. "I never saw anything like it. I am from the year 1401."

"Whatever. Could you leave me alone? I'm in the middle of an important conversation here." Greg walked quickly away from Mark.

Dialogue Tags Other Than "Said"

remembered

replied

roared

sang

screamed

screeched

shouted

sighed

snarled

sobbed

warned

whispered

yelled

It's clear from reading these few lines that Mark and Greg are very different people. Mark has time-traveled from the year 1401 and Greg lives in the present. Greg loves talking on the phone so much that he could care less about meeting a time-traveler!

Also notice that when Mark or Greg's exact words have a dialogue tag, a comma is used instead of an end mark. This is another rule you should follow to make your novel dialogue easy to read.

Comic Strip Exercise

Writing really good dialogue is like writing a comic strip. Comic artists only have so many boxes to fill before they run out of room. If they spend too much time on dialogue like "Hey, dude, how are you?" pretty soon, they've run out of boxes! To help you understand how boring this kind of dialogue can be, we've put together a nifty example of a boring comic strip. Check it out!

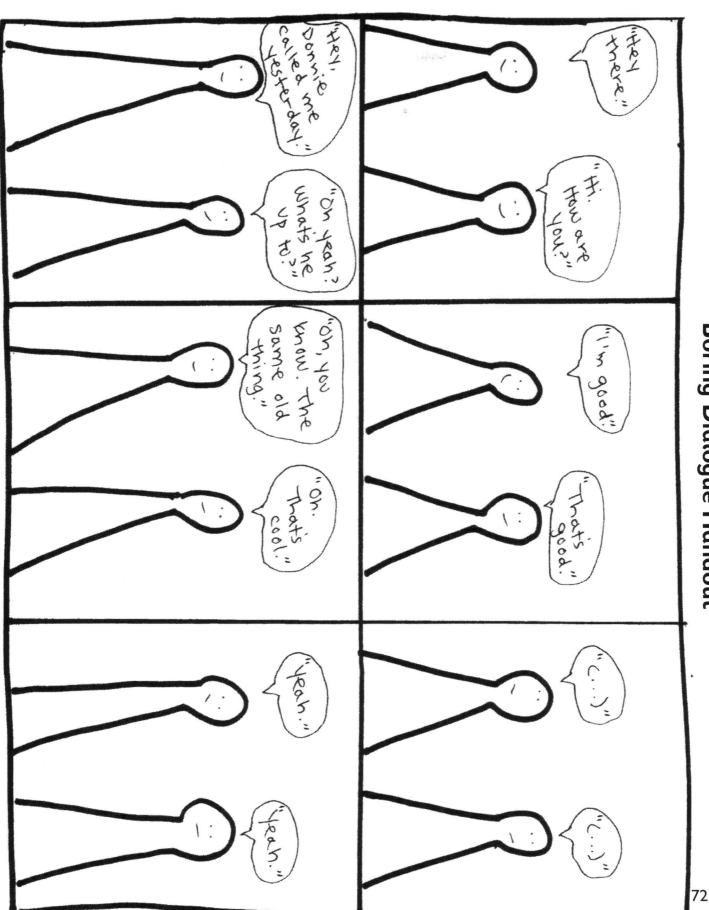

Pretty lame comic, huh? Now it's your turn to write some dialogue that's actually good!

Fill in the following three blank "Comic Strip Worksheets"

1. On the first one, write a conversation between your main character and your villain—they probably have a lot of things to say to each other that will keep a reader's attention! Remember that your dialogue should either move your story forward or help your reader get to know your characters.

2. On the other two, you can either write more conversations between your main character and villain, or you can bring in your supporting characters.

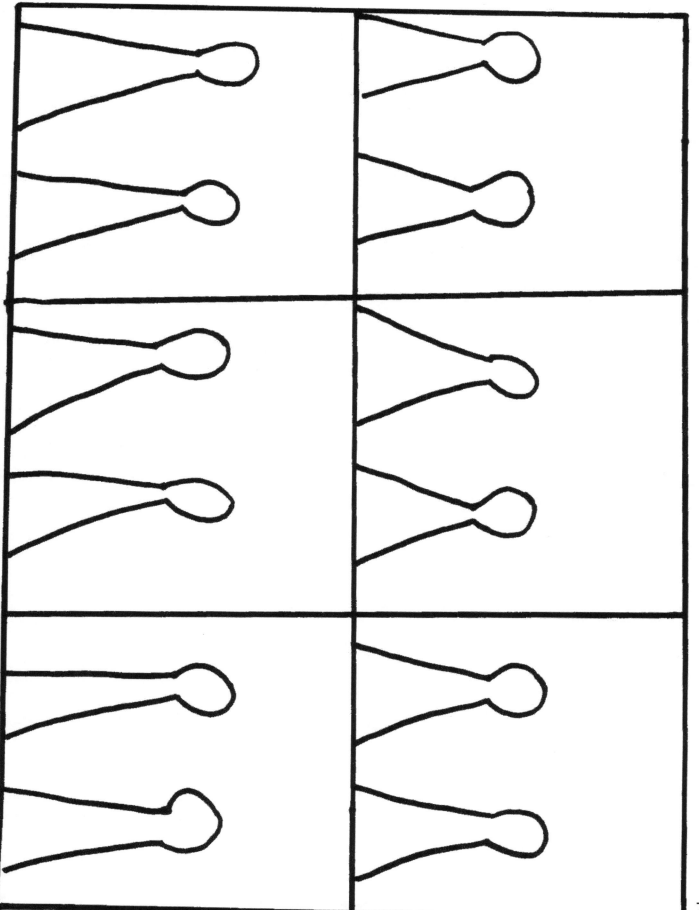

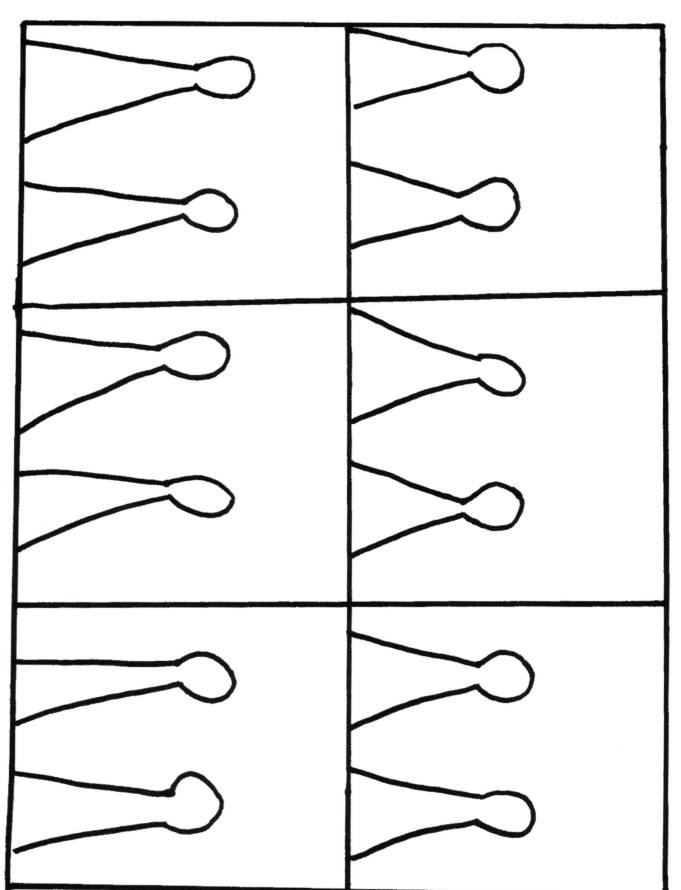

Getting Ready for NaNoWriMo

NaNoWriMo Survival Tips

Now that you know how to write a novel, you may be wondering how you write a novel in just 30 days. Well, we have put together some things that will help you get ready for your noveling adventure. First we would like share with you our **Top Five NaNoWriMo Survival Tips:**

5. **Keep a pile of delicious snacks near your writing station.** That way, if you're having a hard time coming up with ideas, at least you can eat a delicious piece of taffy while you think. If anyone comments on how much candy you've been eating lately, you can just shrug and say "Well, I am writing a novel..."

4. **Move, move, move!** Get out of that chair and stretch your arms and legs! Do a couple of sit-ups or jumping jacks! Go for a bike ride around the block! Challenge your next-door neighbor to an arm-wrestling competition! Keeping your blood moving will keep the ideas flowing, and will ensure you've still got feeling in your rump at the end of November.

3. **Be sure to get plenty of sleep.** Just because you're writing a novel in a month doesn't mean you should neglect catching your Z's. Besides, you never know what kind of interesting characters and settings your dreams might reveal.

2. **Reward yourself.** Every time you reach a word-count milestone, give yourself a reward! Make some popcorn and watch your favorite movie, go lie on a blanket under the stars, grab a megaphone and parade around the neighborhood bragging about how many words you've written so far. You'll be working hard, and you should treat yourself right!

1. **Never say you "can't."** This is the number one thing to remember next month! There are no *can'ts* in month-long novel writing.

You *can* do it.

Remember that tens of thousands of people just like you write a novel in a month every year. No matter how busy you are, or how little you might know about writing a novel, you can finish! If you begin the month thinking you can, you are already way ahead of the game.

National Novel Writing Month Contract

Once you set your word-count goal, fill in and sign this contract. Make sure you get a teacher or parent to sign it, too. If you don't know what goal to set, work with your teacher or parent to set a challenging word-count goal.

NATIONAL NOVEL WRITING MONTH

CONTRACT

I, _____ , hereby pledge my intent to write a

_____ -word novel in one month.

By taking on this crazy month-long challenge, I understand that the ideas of perfect sentences, grammar, and punctuation are to be chucked right out the window, where they will stay until December. I understand that I am a smart person, capable of great acts of creativity, and I will give myself enough time during the next month to allow my talents to come to the surface, without self-bullying.

During the month ahead, I realize I will produce clunky dialogue, boring characters, and bad plots. I agree that all of these things will be left in this first draft, to be corrected at a later point. I understand my right to keep my novel from all readers (except possibly my teacher) until I say so. I also acknowledge my right as an author to brag about how good my novel is and how hard writing it is should such bragging help me gain love, respect, or freedom from household chores.

I acknowledge that the month-long, _____ - word deadline I set for myself is unchangeable. I also acknowledge that, upon finishing the stated writing goal, I get to gleefully celebrate for days, if not weeks, afterward.

_____   _____
YOUR SIGNATURE   DATE

_____   _____
TEACHER/PARENT'S SIGNATURE   DATE

Word-Count Chore Coupons

If you feel like you need more motivation to meet your word-count goal, promise to do unpleasant chores for people if you don't make time to write as much as you should. Below you will find ten chore coupons, one for each **milestone** that you will find on your Triumphant Chart of Noveling Progress on page 85. If you vow to clean out your sister's rat cage if you don't make your first word-count milestone, you better believe you'll make your word count! Get a pair of scissors, cut these out, and give them to people you know.

NANOWRIMO YWP · **CHORE COUPONS**

I _____
YOUR NAME

hereby promise to render _____
CHORE

_____

unto _____
RECIPIENTS NAME

should I fail to write _____
AMOUNT

words of my novel by _____
DATE

X _____
SIGNED   DATE

NANOWRIMO YWP · **CHORE COUPONS**

I _____
YOUR NAME

hereby promise to render _____
CHORE

_____

unto _____
RECIPIENTS NAME

should I fail to write _____
AMOUNT

words of my novel by _____
DATE

X _____
SIGNED   DATE

NANOWRIMO YWP · **CHORE COUPONS**

I _____
YOUR NAME

hereby promise to render _____
CHORE

_____

unto _____
RECIPIENTS NAME

should I fail to write _____
AMOUNT

words of my novel by _____
DATE

X _____
SIGNED   DATE

NANOWRIMO YWP · **CHORE COUPONS**

I _____
YOUR NAME

hereby promise to render _____
CHORE

_____

unto _____
RECIPIENTS NAME

should I fail to write _____
AMOUNT

words of my novel by _____
DATE

X _____
SIGNED   DATE

NANOWRIMO YWP — **CHORE COUPONS**

I _____ YOUR NAME
hereby promise to render _____ CHORE
_____
unto _____ RECIPIENTS NAME
should I fail to write _____ AMOUNT
words of my novel by _____ DATE

X _____
SIGNED   DATE

NANOWRIMO YWP — **CHORE COUPONS**

I _____ YOUR NAME
hereby promise to render _____ CHORE
_____
unto _____ RECIPIENTS NAME
should I fail to write _____ AMOUNT
words of my novel by _____ DATE

X _____
SIGNED   DATE

NANOWRIMO YWP — **CHORE COUPONS**

I _____ YOUR NAME
hereby promise to render _____ CHORE
_____
unto _____ RECIPIENTS NAME
should I fail to write _____ AMOUNT
words of my novel by _____ DATE

X _____
SIGNED   DATE

NANOWRIMO YWP — **CHORE COUPONS**

I _____ YOUR NAME
hereby promise to render _____ CHORE
_____
unto _____ RECIPIENTS NAME
should I fail to write _____ AMOUNT
words of my novel by _____ DATE

X _____
SIGNED   DATE

NANOWRIMO YWP — **CHORE COUPONS**

I _____ YOUR NAME
hereby promise to render _____ CHORE
_____
unto _____ RECIPIENTS NAME
should I fail to write _____ AMOUNT
words of my novel by _____ DATE

X _____
SIGNED   DATE

NANOWRIMO YWP — **CHORE COUPONS**

I _____ YOUR NAME
hereby promise to render _____ CHORE
_____
unto _____ RECIPIENTS NAME
should I fail to write _____ AMOUNT
words of my novel by _____ DATE

X _____
SIGNED   DATE

NaNoWriMo Calendar

Your word-count goal may seem impossible to reach when you look at the huge number of words you have to write in one month. We're here to tell you a secret. **If you break a big goal into smaller daily goals, it will seem a lot less scary.** To help you do this for next month's challenge, we've come up with this NaNoWriMo Calendar.

It is best to set aside time each day to write, but be realistic. If you have soccer practice on Tuesday and Thursday, you may not have time to write those days.

Tip: If you want to find out just how many words you will need to write each day, divide your total word-count by the number of days you can write during the month. For example, if your word-count goal is 1,000, and you can make time to write on 20 days, you will need to write 50 words on each of those days. If this is confusing, ask your teacher to help you with the math!

1

I will write from
_____ TIME AM/PM
to
_____ TIME AM/PM

Word-count goal
for the day
_____ AMOUNT

2

I will write from
_____ TIME AM/PM
to
_____ TIME AM/PM

Word-count goal
for the day
_____ AMOUNT

3

I will write from
_____ TIME AM/PM
to
_____ TIME AM/PM

Word-count goal
for the day
_____ AMOUNT

4

I will write from
_____ TIME AM/PM
to
_____ TIME AM/PM

Word-count goal
for the day
_____ AMOUNT

5

I will write from
_____ TIME AM/PM
to
_____ TIME AM/PM

Word-count goal
for the day
_____ AMOUNT

6

I will write from
_____ TIME AM/PM
to
_____ TIME AM/PM

Word-count goal
for the day
_____ AMOUNT

7

I will write from
_____ TIME AM/PM
to
_____ TIME AM/PM

Word-count goal
for the day
_____ AMOUNT

8

I will write from
_____ TIME AM/PM
to
_____ TIME AM/PM

Word-count goal
for the day
_____ AMOUNT

9

I will write from
_____ TIME AM/PM
to
_____ TIME AM/PM

Word-count goal
for the day
_____ AMOUNT

10

I will write from
_____ TIME AM/PM
to
_____ TIME AM/PM

Word-count goal
for the day
_____ AMOUNT

11

I will write from
_____ TIME AM/PM
to
_____ TIME AM/PM

Word-count goal
for the day
_____ AMOUNT

12

I will write from
_____ TIME AM/PM
to
_____ TIME AM/PM

Word-count goal
for the day
_____ AMOUNT

13

I will write from
_____ TIME AM/PM
to
_____ TIME AM/PM

Word-count goal
for the day
_____ AMOUNT

14

I will write from
_____ TIME AM/PM
to
_____ TIME AM/PM

Word-count goal
for the day
_____ AMOUNT

15

I will write from
_____ TIME AM/PM
to
_____ TIME AM/PM

Word-count goal
for the day
_____ AMOUNT

16

I will write from
_____ TIME AM/PM
to
_____ TIME AM/PM

Word-count goal
for the day
_____ AMOUNT

17

I will write from
_____ TIME AM/PM
to
_____ TIME AM/PM

Word-count goal
for the day
_____ AMOUNT

18

I will write from
_____ TIME AM/PM
to
_____ TIME AM/PM

Word-count goal
for the day
_____ AMOUNT

19

I will write from
_____ TIME AM/PM
to
_____ TIME AM/PM

Word-count goal
for the day
_____ AMOUNT

20

I will write from
_____ TIME AM/PM
to
_____ TIME AM/PM

Word-count goal
for the day
_____ AMOUNT

21

I will write from
_____ TIME AM/PM
to
_____ TIME AM/PM

Word-count goal
for the day
_____ AMOUNT

22

I will write from
_____ TIME AM/PM
to
_____ TIME AM/PM

Word-count goal
for the day
_____ AMOUNT

23

I will write from
_____ TIME AM/PM
to
_____ TIME AM/PM

Word-count goal
for the day
_____ AMOUNT

24

I will write from
_____ TIME AM/PM
to
_____ TIME AM/PM

Word-count goal
for the day
_____ AMOUNT

25

I will write from
_____ TIME AM/PM
to
_____ TIME AM/PM

Word-count goal
for the day
_____ AMOUNT

26

I will write from
_____ TIME AM/PM
to
_____ TIME AM/PM

Word-count goal
for the day
_____ AMOUNT

27

I will write from
_____ TIME AM/PM
to
_____ TIME AM/PM

Word-count goal
for the day
_____ AMOUNT

28

I will write from
_____ TIME AM/PM
to
_____ TIME AM/PM

Word-count goal
for the day
_____ AMOUNT

29

I will write from
_____ TIME AM/PM
to
_____ TIME AM/PM

Word-count goal
for the day
_____ AMOUNT

30

I will write from
_____ TIME AM/PM
to
_____ TIME AM/PM

Word-count goal
for the day
_____ AMOUNT

Ready, Set, Write . . . And Keep Writing!

NaNoWriMo's Personal
Chart of Noveling Progress

Write your word-count goal at the top of the page, and color this chart in as you write! If you don't know what numbers to write in at each milestone, ask your teacher or parent to help you with the math.

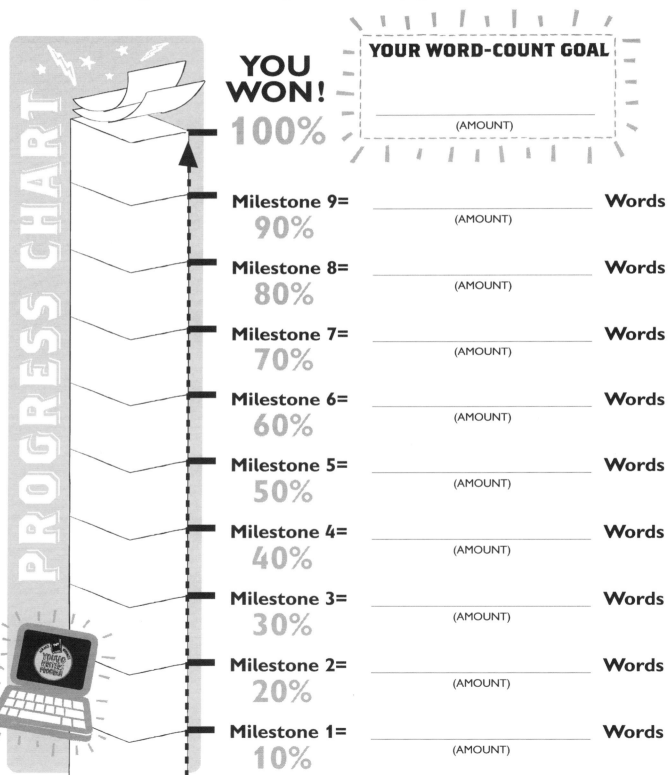

PROGRESS CHART

YOU WON! 100%

YOUR WORD-COUNT GOAL

_____
(AMOUNT)

Milestone 9= 90% _____ **Words**
(AMOUNT)

Milestone 8= 80% _____ **Words**
(AMOUNT)

Milestone 7= 70% _____ **Words**
(AMOUNT)

Milestone 6= 60% _____ **Words**
(AMOUNT)

Milestone 5= 50% _____ **Words**
(AMOUNT)

Milestone 4= 40% _____ **Words**
(AMOUNT)

Milestone 3= 30% _____ **Words**
(AMOUNT)

Milestone 2= 20% _____ **Words**
(AMOUNT)

Milestone 1= 10% _____ **Words**
(AMOUNT)

Start at the Beginning!

Here it is, the first day of November, and you're ready to start your NaNo-adventure! But you might be wondering where to begin. Well, at the beginning, of course!

So, you've already got a cast of interesting characters, an adventure-packed plot, some amazing settings, and the know-how to write some really good dialogue. Now, you just need a beginning.

Before you start writing your own first sentence, it might be a good idea to read some other first sentences. That way, you will get an idea of all the possibilities out there in the first-sentence world!

Good first sentences are all alike in some ways. First, they usually help to introduce a novel's plot or part of the plot, even in a tiny way. Second, they include exciting details or descriptions that make people want to keep reading. First sentences can be different, too.

They can be:

- Funny.

- Scary.

- Sad.

- Magical (or filled with fantasy like *Harry Potter* or *The Chronicles of Narnia*).

- Realistic (or about things that happen in your everyday life).

We've gone ahead and written a couple of first sentences for you to check out. As you read each one, think about how it includes details about what the book's plot might be and whether it makes you want to keep reading. Then try to decide what kind of a novel you think it belongs to. There are no right or wrong answers—in fact, you may find that some of these first lines are both funny and magical, or sad and realistic.

Check all the boxes that you think describe each sentence below:

"When I woke up there was a giant green bunny standing at the foot of my bed, and he did not look happy."
- ☐ Funny
- ☐ Scary
- ☐ Sad
- ☐ Magical
- ☐ Realistic

"It was a dark and stormy night."
- ☐ Funny
- ☐ Scary
- ☐ Sad
- ☐ Magical
- ☐ Realistic

"I know it sounds easy, but trust me, slaying dragons is hard work!"
- ☐ Funny
- ☐ Scary
- ☐ Sad
- ☐ Magical
- ☐ Realistic

"When Captain Smith and his men landed on Mars, the first thing they noticed was the awful smell."
- ☐ Funny
- ☐ Scary
- ☐ Sad
- ☐ Magical
- ☐ Realistic

"When our dog Pluto died last May, I was sure that nothing was ever going to be the same again."
- ☐ Funny
- ☐ Scary
- ☐ Sad
- ☐ Magical
- ☐ Realistic

"With cheerleading tryouts just four days away, Amanda was starting to get nervous."

- ☐ Funny
- ☐ Scary
- ☐ Sad
- ☐ Magical
- ☐ Realistic

Now it's time for you to try writing some first sentences. We've gone ahead and started a few, and we need your help to finish them!

FINISH THIS SCARY FIRST LINE

"There was a sound coming from the dark basement, and it sounded like..."

_____

_____

_____

FINISH THIS FUNNY FIRST LINE

"Every Monday something goes terribly wrong, like all of a sudden there are monkeys in..."

_____

_____

_____

FINISH THIS SAD FIRST LINE

"Rain always made Max think of the time that ..."

_____

_____

_____

FINISH THIS FANTASTICAL FIRST LINE

"The thing that everyone should know about forest elves is..."

_____

_____

_____

FINISH THIS REALISTIC FIRST LINE

"I'm not going to school today because..."

_____

_____

_____

All right! Now that your brain is all warmed up, it's time to dive right into your novel!

From the list below, decide what kind of novel you think yours is going to be. (Remember, it can be more than one!) Then, write your first sentence on your computer or in your notebook.

My novel is:
- ☐ Funny.
- ☐ Scary.
- ☐ Sad.
- ☐ Magical.
- ☐ Realistic.

Write with All Your Senses!

A great way to boost your word count during NaNoWriMo is by adding more **description** to your story. A great way to do this is by using your five senses:

 1. Taste

 2. Touch

 3. Smell

 4. Sight

 5. Hearing

"Gary is eating an ice cream sundae." = 7 words!

"Gary is eating a mouth-watering vanilla, chocolate, and strawberry sundae. The hot fudge on top smells like heaven, and is melting the cold ice cream. Gary is eating the sundae so fast he is making slurping noises, which is making his mom angry. He has whipped cream all over his face, but Gary doesn't care. It's the most delicious thing he's ever eaten in his whole life." = 67 words!

Wow, who knew a pretend ice cream sundae could do so much for your word count?

Below, we've listed a couple of things that need more details. Practice writing with your five senses by answering the questions about each item. The more words you use to describe each, the better! Also, feel free to use all the cool words you'll find in the "Word Bank" boxes below.

A birthday cake

What color is the cake? Is there a special design on the cake?

_____

_____

_____

What flavor is the cake? The frosting?

_____

_____

_____

Does it smell good?

_____

_____

_____

If you touched it, what would it feel like?

_____

_____

_____

> **Word Bank for "Nice"**
>
> delightful,
> kind,
> likable,
> pleasant,
> charming,
> agreeable,
> friendly,
> gracious,
> polite

A carnival

What sounds can be heard at a carnival?

_____

_____

_____

What strange and interesting things are there to see?

_____

_____

_____

Is there anything delicious to eat?

_____

_____

_____

Word Bank for "Awesome"

amazing,
extraordinary,
outstanding,
incredible,
magnificent,
wonderful,
superb,
fantastic,
spectacular

What do you smell at a carnival?

_____

Your main character has never been on a rollercoaster.
Can you tell him what it feels like?

_____

_____

A rainstorm

What does the rain feel like on your skin?

_____

_____

What does the air smell like?

_____

_____

Do you hear anything?

_____

_____

What do the clouds look like?

_____

_____

What does a raindrop taste like?

_____

_____

93

A busy city street

What kind of sounds do you hear?

_____

_____

_____

What smells are in the air?

_____

_____

_____

What do you see around you?

_____

_____

_____

There's a man selling food from a cart. What is it? What does it taste like?

_____

_____

_____

Word Bank for "Bad"

ghastly, dreadful, terrible, appalling, horrific, awful, abominable, disastrous

A beach

What sounds do you hear?

_____

_____

_____

Word Bank for "Good"

excellent,
superior,
outstanding,
fantastic,
terrific,
marvelous,
exceptional,
incredible

What kinds of things are there to eat?

_____

_____

What do you smell?

_____

_____

What does the sand feel like on your skin?

_____

_____

How about the water? How does it feel?

_____

_____

An old pair of socks

What do they look like?

_____

_____

_____

What do they feel like?

_____

_____

_____

What do they smell like? (Ewwww!)

_____

_____

_____

What do they taste like? (Double ewwww!)

_____

_____

_____

Now, when you go back to your book, make sure you add as many details as you can by using **taste, touch, smell, sight, and hearing**. That way, people will know how gross your villain's old socks really are!

Character Interviews on NaNo-TV

One super-helpful way to get to know your characters even more than you already do is by stepping into his or her shoes. . . or hat, or sunglasses. Grab an article of clothing that each of your three characters might wear, and get ready, because we've got news for you—they've all been invited to be interviewed on NaNo-TV!

For this TV interview, you'll need to dress like your characters dress, to think like your characters think, and to talk like your characters talk! Imagining, for a little while, that you are the characters you've created is one of the best ways to get to know them. Plus, after these interviews, you may discover interesting plot twists that you hadn't thought of yet!

With a friend or by yourself, answer the interview questions as though you were your characters.

MAIN CHARACTER INTERVIEW

Host: Hello, _____ , and welcome to the show! We're really excited to
       (your main character's name)
have you here today. Can you tell us a little about what is going on in your life right now?

Main Character:

_____

_____

_____

Host: Wow! It sounds like you have a lot going on. Rumor has it, though, that someone is out to get you. We've heard you've been having some trouble with a villain. Can you tell us a little about what that villain is up to these days?

Main Character:

_____

_____

_____

_____

_____

Host: Yes, sounds villainous indeed! Do you have any idea why this villain is so mean all the time?

Main Character:

_____

_____

_____

_____

Host: That makes sense. Do you have anyone who has been helping you out throughout your adventure? A supporting character, perhaps? What has he or she been doing lately?

Main Character:

_____

_____

_____

_____

_____

Host: You're lucky to have that person/animal/talking toaster by your side. We've all been wondering, and we hope you'll tell the folks at home—would you rather be able to fly, or have the ability to become invisible, and why?

Main Character:

_____

_____

_____

_____

_____

Host: A wise choice! Before we go, why don't you tell the audience your three greatest wishes in the entire world?

Main Character:

_____

_____

_____

_____

_____

_____

Host: Those are some fantastic wishes! It's been a real pleasure to have you on the show. We hope you'll come back soon. Up next, we'll get the inside track on the supporting character, just after this short commercial break. Don't go away!

Okay, now it's time for your supporting character to be interviewed! Switch out your main character outfit for something your supporting character would wear. Does your supporting character always wear a crazy hat? Or a pair of sunglasses that your main character wouldn't wear in a million years? Put on your special supporting character item, and get ready to be interviewed!

SUPPORTING CHARACTER INTERVIEW

Host: Hello, _____ , and welcome to the show! We were just
       (your supporting character's name)
speaking to the main character about his or her three biggest wishes. Why don't you tell us about your three biggest wishes? Are they any different from the main character's wishes?

Supporting Character:

_____

_____

_____

_____

_____

_____

Host: Interesting. Do you have any special skills that might help?

Supporting Character:

_____

_____

_____

_____

_____

_____

Host: Sounds great! Hey, it looks like we've got a call coming through. Hello, you're on NaNo-TV, the best TV show on the planet. What's your question?

Caller: _Yes, hi. I've been dying to ask you this question since the show began. Do you, um, do you like cats or dogs more? And why?_

Supporting Character:

_____

_____

_____

_____

_____

Host: Thanks for the question, caller. Now, is there anything that you're excited or nervous about for the upcoming adventures you face?

Supporting Character:

_____

_____

_____

_____

_____

Host: Well, we wish you all the best of luck in supporting the main character, and we look forward to hearing how things pan out for you. One last question before we bring in the villain for an interview. Let's pretend you had to choose between eating pizza for the rest of your life, or ice cream. Which would you choose?

Supporting Character:

_____

_____

_____

_____

_____

_____

Host: Wow! That's a bold choice! Thank you so much for your time. We hope you'll join us again soon. Up next: the dangerous, the scheming, the evil villain right here on our show! Don't go away!

Okay, now it's time to put on your most wicked outfit to think like your villain, to plan evil plans like your villain, and to be the most monstrous villain you can be! Get out your villain hat or cape or villain disco pants, and get ready to be interviewed!

VILLAIN INTERVIEW

Host: Hi, _____ , and welcome to the show! How did you become
         (your villain's name)
so villainous? Have you always been this way?

Villain:

_____

_____

_____

_____

Host: You're very villainous indeed! We've just spoken to the main character and the supporting character, and they've told us a little about how you are trying to stand in their way. Would you like to give your side of the story?

Villain:

_____

_____

_____

_____

Host: Fascinating. Why are you and the main character enemies? What happened? Were you ever friends?

Villain:

_____

_____

_____

_____

Host: Very interesting! Could you take a moment and tell the studio audience about your three biggest wishes in the world?

Villain:

_____

_____

_____

_____

_____

Host: Wow, you really are a villain, in every way. Well, we can't say we wish you luck, but we do look forward to hearing how things turn out. We hope you'll come back again and join us when November is over. Oh, before you go, a question that's on everyone's minds: How much do you love kittens? A little bit, a whole lot, or not at all?

Villain:

_____

_____

_____

_____

Host: Yes, I thought you might say that. Well, thank you for your time. It's been really great having all three characters on the show. And to all our audience members out there in TV land, we hope you'll join us tomorrow, when I'll be wrestling an alligator, blind-folded. See you soon!

Lists! Lists! Lists!

Here's a cool activity to boost your word count—make a list or two! Lists are great, because they're a good way to give your brain a little break from all that noveling, and they also let you get to know your characters in ways you didn't think of before. After you make a list about a character, you just take the things in your list, put it paragraph form, and, just like that, you've added some awesome details to your novel. And added to your word count!

A list of things my main character likes to do on Saturdays:

1. Eat strawberry pie

2. Watch re-runs of cartoons

3. Go on bike rides

4. Buy lemonade from the kid down the block

5. Practice the banjo

6. Eat more strawberry pie

7. Take the dog on a walk to the park

And now, in paragraph form:
Larry loved Saturdays! They were a great chance for him to relax and do all the things he didn't get time for during the week. Every Saturday morning, Larry woke up early and ate some strawberry pie. Then, he watched some re-runs of old cartoons, then took a bike ride, and, while he was out, he bought some lemonade from the kid down the block. He came home to practice his banjo, then he ate more strawberry pie before taking the dog on a walk to the park. Nothing compared to a Saturday for Larry.

All right, now it's your turn! Fill out the lists below about your characters. After you finish a list, you can write it into your novel in paragraph form:

1. Things underneath my main character's bed.

_____

_____

_____

_____

_____

_____

2. What my main character likes to do on the weekend.

_____

_____

_____

_____

_____

_____

3. Things my main character collects.

_____

_____

_____

_____

_____

_____

_____

4. Things in my villain's refrigerator.

_____

_____

_____

_____

_____

_____

5. Things my villain likes to do on the weekend.

_____

_____

_____

_____

_____

6. Things hanging on my villain's bedroom wall.

_____

_____

_____

_____

_____

If you get stuck at all during NaNoWriMo, just come back to these lists. You can do them all at once or one at a time. After you fill one out, remember that you can rewrite it into your novel in paragraph form.

I Wrote a Novel! Now What?

The Workshop

Today your novel will be read for the very first time by someone other than you! Fortunately, that person is also a novelist. He or she knows what you've been through in the last month and will have a lot of useful tips on how to improve your work. You will do the same for him or her, too.

Below are guidelines you and your partner will follow as you read one another's novels.

• **Read the draft once without writing anything.** Then read it again and write your ideas and questions on the side.

• **Forget about grammar, spelling, and how you would say something if it were your novel.** Today, focus on the story—the characters, the events, the setting, and your partner's awesome writing.

• **Take time to circle words, sentences, or whole sections that you really like.** Then, on the side, write a short sentence describing what you liked about each one.

• **Ask lot of questions.** If something doesn't make sense, ask about it. If you need more detail about a character, ask about it. If you just want to know how your partner came up with a word, phrase, or idea, ask about it!

• **Be kind, and specific, as you point out things you don't love.** "This paragraph is really long" is much more helpful than "I don't like this paragraph."

To get an idea of what "helpful" comments are, compare these two paragraphs.

Not So Helpful

"Stop, thief!" Ann cried. People stared as the guy took off with her backpack. Ann panicked. She had to get that pack back! What would she tell Juan when she got to their meeting spot without it? And without the magic stone inside, how would they travel back in time to stop Mt. Toppopoffolis from erupting and destroying their whole town?

I don't get it

??

I like your writing.

Unfortunately, like a boring novel, these comments lack detail. It's hard to tell what the reader is confused about in the first sentence, or why he or she wrote question marks a few lines later. And the last comment, "I like your writing," doesn't let the writer know what he/she is specifically doing well.

Helpful!

"Stop, thief!" Ann cried. People stared as the guy took off with her backpack. Ann panicked. She had to get that pack back! What would she tell Juan when she got to their meeting spot without it? And without the magic stone inside, how would they travel back in time to stop Mt. Toppopoffolis from erupting and destroying their whole town?

It's not clear where this scene takes place

Did you rhyme on purpose? Nice!

Very mysterious. I want to read more!

These comments are more helpful because they are specific. Now the writer knows what he or she needs to fix and what he or she is already doing well.

Reader Review Worksheet

Take out your partner's draft and fill in the blanks below. And remember, be specific! Return this sheet to your partner when you are done.

Your partner's name: _____

Novel Title: _____

1. Based on the beginning, what do you think this novel is about?

_____

_____

_____

2. Who is the most important character so far? What is he or she like?

_____

_____

_____

3. Where is the story set? Would you like more detail? If so, what part of the setting would you like to know more about?

_____

_____

_____

4. List two things you really like about your partner's work so far.

_____

_____

_____

_____

5. List two things your partner can work on as he or she revises.

_____

_____

_____

_____

Unleash Your Inner Editor

NaNoWriMo is over! Can you believe it? Well, it doesn't have to be completely over. Now you can revise your novel. "Revise" is just a fancy word for making changes and corrections to make your novel even better.

You've gotten some helpful editing notes from classmates so far, but you still need more information. You need to decide what you think about your writing. Begin by reading the first three to five pages of your novel. Chances are, you haven't looked at these in a while! What surprises you? What impresses you? Fill in the box below to explain what you notice about your writing. If you get stuck, think of comments from your workshop partners. You can also look at the sample below.

> **My novel is**
> *different from what I expected when I started writing.*
>
> **I can't believe**
> *I came up with such a great character on the very first day.*

My novel is

_____

_____

I can't believe I

_____

_____

Now use your draft to answer the questions below.

Note: You may notice that none of the questions have to do with grammar or spelling mistakes. You and your Inner Editor will fix those last, after you've revised your writing in every other way.

1. Turn to a page where one chapter ends and another begins, and/or find a section where you change settings. Tell about some linking words you used between paragraphs and events to make the order of events clear.

_____

_____

_____

2. Name two changes you plan to make as you revise your writing so the order of events is clearer. These changes could be big (moving events around) or small (adding words like "then" to make the order clearer).

• _____

• _____

3. Think about the mood, or feeling, of the beginning of your novel. How do you want the first few pages to sound? You may circle more than one thing and/or even add your own.

• Funny

• Dark or scary

• Sad

• Like science fiction or fantasy

• Happy

• Mysterious

• Exciting

• Other: _____

• Other: _____

• Other: _____

4. Name two ways you can make this feeling even stronger. Your changes may be big (such as adding a whole new event), or small (such as adding a few adjectives).

• _____

• _____

5. In two sentences, describe your main character and what is special about him or her.

_____

_____

_____

_____

6. Describe one or two of the other important characters.

_____

_____

_____

_____

_____

7. Name two changes you plan to make that might make your main character or other characters more interesting. For example, you may add details about his or her past, or have the character do something unusual that helps readers understand him or her.

• _____

• _____

8. Which of these did you use a lot of in your first few pages? (Circle all that apply to your novel.)

• Dialogue

• Sensory detail about settings

• Sensory detail about characters

9. Name three ways you can revise your writing to add dialogue or sensory detail. These changes could be big (add dialogue everywhere) or small (add two or three adjectives to a certain character description in the second paragraph of page two).

• _____

• _____

• _____

Finally, check out the directions and example below. They show how to take the changes you wrote about above and mark them on your novel.

When editing your novel, you should:

• Cross out words or sentences you want to get rid of.

• Write notes to yourself in the white space around your story.

• Use circles and arrows to show how you want to add or move words.

Lewis sat up in bed. What was that noise? He heard a small tapping sound. It's probably just a chipmunk, Lewis told himself, and put his head back on his pillow. A minute passed before he heard the tapping again, though. It was getting louder. That's when he saw it— a big giant shadow moving in the moonlight. That's no chipmunk, Lewis thought to himself. It looks more like a polar bear! It was coming towards his window.

Just outside his window,

Only

Okay, now you have a plan for revising your writing. But before you start, you'll need to go get your Inner Editor from the secret, faraway place where you hid him a month ago. Once you have him, paste him in the space below:

Inner Editor: (Brushing the dust from his or her sleeves) Hrmf! Thank you for bringing me back! It looks like you just wrote an entire novel without my help. Though I am a little mad about being ignored for over a month, I understand that I would have made writing a whole book in a month really hard.

You: Thanks for understanding!

Inner Editor: (picking up your novel and beginning to read) Well, let me see here. Wow, this novel is really good. That is impossible! Did you borrow some else's Inner Editor last month?

You: Nope. I did all on my own. I had a lot of fun without you, but I am ready to revise my novel (and I have a few spelling tests coming up), so I thought I would bring you back out to help me get started.

Inner Editor: I can't believe it. You're a real novelist! Well, I guess I can help. Revising a novel is fun, but it isn't easy. You definitely need me now!

Cleaning It Up

All month long, we've told you to focus on getting your words on paper. "Don't worry if it's not perfect," we've said repeatedly. Now we take it back! You've worked really hard on this novel, and while it doesn't have to be perfect, you also don't want it to be full of typos. Typos and grammar mistakes make it hard for readers to pay attention to your awesome story.

Read the description of each writing mistake below. Then grab your very best red pen, imagine it's a scrub-brush, and clean up the messy sentences!

Tricksters

First, check your spelling. But don't think you can count on your computer's spell check. Spell check won't pick up on tricky words that sound alike, such as "they're," "their," and "there." You've got to use your own brain to find those mistakes!

> It seemed like a good idea the night before. But now as Simon walked into homeroom, he new heed maid a mistake. He nevur should have let his brother cut his hare.

Of course if you get stumped by a word, try looking it up in the dictionary. This is a great way to double-check tricky spellings.

Beginning and End

Use correct capitalization and punctuation including commas, semicolons, quotation marks, apostrophes, and end marks.

> The first person to say something was his pal Luis Geez simon whats going on with your hair?

Make Your Mark!

Mark	Meaning
∧	insert
⌐	delete
⌇	switch
⊙	period
⋀	comma
ⱴ	quotation marks
⫪	start new paragraph

Pick and Stick

Use past tense, present tense, and future tenses correctly. Most importantly, pick one tense and stick to it.

> Simon turns bright red. He quickly put his baseball cap on so no one else sees his hair. Unfortunately, his teacher saw his hat.
> "Simon, you knew the rules about hats in class! Take it off!"

We Agree

Make sure all your subjects and verbs agree. Also make sure you use pronouns correctly.

> Simon took his hat off, hoping no one were looking. But it were too late. One by one, Simon's classmates turned to stare at he.

Mix It Up!

Make sure all your sentences are complete, each including both a subject and a verb. Also keep your writing interesting by using different sentence lengths and types. You can use words *like* and *to* connect sentences when necessary.

> Simon's teacher giggled. Luis giggled. His classmates giggled. Even Pufferton the class hamster giggled. Simon had never been so embarrassed.

The Right Word

Make sure to use describing words correctly. Words that describe verbs often end in —ly. Words that describe nouns do not end in —ly.

> Simon sat down slow. He couldn't stop thinking about how his brother tricked him. Now he looked ridiculously! He would get back at his brother, oh yes he would.

Now that you know how to proofread like a pro, apply this Inner Editor Proofreading Checklist to your own novel!

☐ Every sentence begins with a capital letter.

☐ Every proper noun begins with a capital letter.

☐ Every sentence has the correct end mark.

☐ I use other punctuation marks such as commas, semicolons, apostrophes, and quotation marks correctly.

☐ I use different kinds of sentences and combined sentences where I could.

☐ All my subjects and verbs agree.

☐ I use pronouns and describing words correctly.

☐ I have checked my spelling.

☐ I have *really* checked my spelling and checked tricky words in the dictionary.

After you check off all of the following, and you feel good about your book, go to the "Resources" section on the NaNoWriMo YWP site (http://ywp.nanowrimo.org) for opportunities to publish your book, submit to contests, and continue your brilliant writing career!

Made in the USA
Lexington, KY
20 September 2018